The Cheese Mall

Key Marketing Skills for the Budding Entrepreneur

By Bernie Tracey

Published By
Beacon Coaching Consultancy
Kildare, Ireland

Copyright © 2011 by Bernie Tracey

All rights reserved. No part of this book may be reproduced or transmitted in any form or by any means, electronic or mechanical, without written permission from the author. Thank you for respecting the work of this author.

A catalogue record for this book is available from the British Library

Copies are available at special rates for bulk orders. For more information, please email the sales team at info@beaconcoaching.ie

Cover illustration Derry Dillon Illustrations, Carlow, Ireland

Dedication

This book is dedicated to all the decent hardworking entrepreneurs out there who everyday make a difference in people's lives.

Table of Contents

INTRODUCTION..1

CHAPTER 1:
The Day Everything Changed..........................3

CHAPTER 2:
Getting Started..8

CHAPTER 3:
The Business Plan..18

CHAPTER 4:
The Marketing Audit.......................................24

CHAPTER 5:
Market Segmentation.....................................31

CHAPTER 6:
Building a Brand...43

CHAPTER 7:
Marketing Communications............................49

CHAPTER 8
Strategic Objectives.......................................62

CHAPTER 9
The Day of Reckoning....................................68

INTRODUCTION

What is marketing really all about? This is the most difficult question for people to answer when they are starting a business.

People think that marketing is about brochures, websites and advertising spend. Of course these are important, but really effective marketing goes beyond that.

When you are starting a business, you need to try to imagine what your business is going to look like in three years' time. Once you have created that vision, you can work backwards from this. Understanding where you want to be will help you figure out HOW you are going to get there.

We all know that we cannot make a journey without a destination in mind. If we start out on the road to running a business and we have no idea where we are heading, how will we know when we have arrived?

This simple marketing book will take the mystery out of marketing. It tells the story of Millie and Matthew, two young entrepreneurial mice who have been made redundant and decide to start up their own shop called The Cheese Mall in a very competitive environment.

The book follows Millie and Matthew on their journey and explores key marketing principles that are easy to understand and follow. The core message of The Cheese Mall is that marketing is all about serving the customer and putting them at the centre of everything you do.

In this book, you will look at your own business through the eyes of Millie and Matthew and share their fears and excitement about being their own boss and starting their own business.

If you are already in business, it will help you take a fresh look at your own business model and ask yourself some basic questions like: 'What am I all about as a business?' and 'How can I give the best possible service to my customer?'

Those of you who are starting out on your entrepreneurial journey will be able to relate to Millie and Matthew and they will guide you every step of the way, giving you a road map to help you reach your destination.

CHAPTER 1
The Day Everything Changed

Millie woke earlier than her twin Matthew and prepared her usual cheese breakfast. Her Dad had already gone to work at the Cheese Factory in Mouseville - even after thirty years of working with the company, he still wanted to make a good impression. Millie greatly admired her Dad and she had been delighted when he had managed to get jobs for herself and Matthew at the Cheese Factory. However, after just one year, she was tiring of the same routine, day in, day out.

Matthew felt the same way. They were beginning to feel trapped, as their Dad kept reminding them that the Cheese Factory was a job for life. This depressed Millie but she kept her spirits high because she had plans to one day run her own business.

She was a little concerned about Matthew lately. He was becoming very restless and Millie was afraid that he might just walk out of the Cheese Factory. Her Dad would go ballistic. She knew that Matthew also had his dreams of being his own boss one day. Their Dad always encouraged them in whatever they wanted to do, but he did not believe they would ever take a risk like that.

Matthew appeared in the doorway, late again and grabbed a cheese sandwich. Off they went to work. Their Mum waved them off from her bedroom window and they could both see how proud she was that her two children had secured plum jobs with the biggest employer in Mouseville and the leading cheese distributor in the whole country. Matthew and Millie walked in silence - neither of them were morning mice.

When they arrived at work, there was an unusual buzz about the place. The security mouse told them that there was going to be a big meeting and all the head mice were going to be there. Matthew was delighted that at least their day was not going to be the same as yesterday but Millie sensed that something bad was about to happen.

They spotted their Dad driving up and down the warehouse, loading cartons of cheese on to the big trucks for the main cities. He looked worried, but tried to smile as he waved over at them.

Matthew said goodbye to Millie and made his way to the IT Department, while she went to her desk in the Customer Service Department.

Nobody was working in her department - every mouse was whispering to each other. Millie read the notice on her desk which said that there was to be a general meeting of all staff in the main boardroom at 10.00 – one hour's time.

Everybody was looking in Millie's direction. They felt it was inevitable that she would be first to go, because she was last in so to speak.

The company grapevine moved quickly into action. They were going to be letting 200 mice go and Millie knew that both she and Matthew would be at the top of the list. Millie understood and accepted this, even though she was one of the best workers and a regular recipient of the 'Mouse Employee of the Month' award, but rules were rules. Matthew sent her an email.

"Looks like we'll be the first to go," he wrote. "It's a relief, but I know Dad will be devastated."

At 09.50, all the mice in the Cheese Factory made their way towards the main boardroom.

It was a tight squeeze and some of them could not fit in, so they stood in the corridor. "The news is bad," the CEO confirmed. "Sales are down, profits are dropping, costs are increasing and demand for our cheddar cheese is declining because of increased imports of specialist cheese. We need to make some savings so we can survive this crisis."

He went on to say that 200 mice would be made redundant from every area of the business. "Last in, first out – it's the only fair way." There were gasps of horror all round.

Some mice cried, others were silent and others felt relieved that, given their tenure, they would not be affected by the announcement. Although Millie was not very keen on her job, the idea of not having it anymore made her feel more stressed than she had ever felt before.

She looked over at Matthew, who was also looking serious. But it was her Dad's face that she would never forget. He wasn't upset because he was losing his job, but because his children were going to be without a job. He knew there was no hope that they would find a similar role in Mouseville and the thought of them leaving would just be too much for him and their mother to bear.

Millie made up her mind right there and then. She walked over to Matthew and said to him:

"This is the day our lives change forever."

"What do you mean?" Matthew replied.

"There's no other choice for us, Matthew. We're just going to have to start our own business and create our own destiny."

Matthew smiled brightly at her, safe in the knowledge that they could make a real go of it together. He had absolutely no idea what they could possibly do, but he was willing to give it his best shot.

They both smiled over at their Dad. As they made their way towards him, he saw something in their eyes that he had not seen in a long time, real excitement.

CHAPTER 2
Getting Started

Leaving the Cheese Factory was easy for Millie and Matthew. Because they had only worked there for a year, the redundancy money was not great, but it would keep them going for a couple of weeks. They started looking at business opportunities within the town, but had to be realistic. Because they had no capital to speak of, their options were limited.

They understood that the purpose of a business is to make a profit and manage this profit efficiently. They also understood that the success of their business would be determined by their ability to adapt rapidly to the ever changing external business environment.

They could see that the Cheese Factory did not respond quickly to what was going on in their market and that was why they got themselves into so much trouble. They hadn't listened to what their customers wanted and didn't respond fast enough to competitor activity and to external market forces.

Millie and Matthew came up with the idea of setting up a Cheese Mall in Mouseville. They saw a gap in the market for a specialised cheese outlet which offered more than just cheese products. They were both very excited about this and felt that this was exactly what the market wanted because there was nothing like it in Mouseville.

Most of the stores tended to be the same and if one store got a new product in, you could be sure that by the end of the week all the stores in the town would have it. But what they had in mind was different and would not be so easy to copy.

"Hold on a second, Millie," said Matthew. "Before we get too excited about this concept, we have to ask the market first."

"What do you mean?" Millie replied.

"Well, we think this will work and we're going to convince the Mice People's Bank it will work, but we haven't asked the 'market' if it will work. Remember what happened in the Cheese Factory; they just went on producing the same old reliable cheese because they thought there was a market for it."

"You're right, Matthew. When the specialist cheeses came in from overseas, they were hit on all sides by an ever growing competitor base."

"Millie, what really happened to them was they didn't listen or ask their customers what they wanted; they just continued producing what they wanted to produce because it was economically viable for them to do so."

"Yes I know," Millie sighed.

"Their customers wanted specialist cheese, not the standard cheddar type. I mean, how dumb is that? How can a company be so out of touch with their customers?"

"So Matthew, what you're saying is we need to do some **Market Research** so that we can prove to the Mice People's Bank that the market would be very receptive to our Cheese Mall. So the market, which is essentially our target customers, needs to be researched, so that we can be totally assured that this is what they need."

"Yes, that's what I'm getting at."

"You are absolutely right, Matthew. How can we possibly convince the Bank that there is a market for what we want to do when we have no research evidence to support it? Leave it with me; I will find out what the steps are and what we need to do to carry out market research."

Millie spent the next two days drawing up a **Market Research Plan** with four key stages, which she presented to Matthew. Firstly, they needed to define the market opportunities and their research objectives. In their case, the market opportunities centred on the demand for a specialist retail cheese outlet in Mouseville and their research objectives were to prove this demand and gather as much information as possible on their target market to support their findings.

Secondly, they had to decide what market information they needed and how they were going to get this information. In their case, they needed to look at their competitors, previous buying trends and what was happening in the present with regard to customer preferences. They needed to anticipate the future needs of their customers, which Millie explained would be the hardest part of the research, because it is always difficult to predict trends.

Thirdly, they needed to gather **Primary Data**. This was new information which could be obtained directly from the target market through Focus Groups (8-10 people), Personal Interviews, and Telephone or Postal surveys.

Fourthly, they needed to look at **Secondary Data** (research reports, Internet, newspapers). Millie explained that this information would already be available and that they could access it easily to help them understand their external market environment.

There were two types of information which they needed to gather. One was called **Quantitative Data**, which referred to how many customers they would have, how much money these customers were likely to spend and where they were currently spending their money.

It was important that they got a figure for the target market's overall spending on specialised cheese. This would provide raw facts and figures for the Bank, which the Bank preferred because they based their decision on this information.

The second type of information was called **Qualitative Data**, which looked at attitudes and opinions and explained why mice prefer one shop over another or one product over another.

Matthew and Millie worked long hours to put the Market Research Plan together. They knew their findings would be critical in convincing the Mice People's Bank to loan them the money for the store. They made a list of places where they could look for the **Secondary Data**.

Their list included the Central Statistics Office, Business and Trade Publications (Mouse Retail magazine), Government Departments (Department of Agriculture), State Agencies (Mouse Enterprise Board), Local Authorities, Published Annual Reports from their competitors, Internet User Groups & Special Interest Groups and Competitor Websites. They did not realise how much information (secondary data) was available and could see the real value of gathering this data in order to put a business case to the Bank.

Regarding the **Primary Data**, Millie decided that a Mouse Focus Group would be beneficial. She planned to include a mix of working and stay at home mouse mums, professionals, elderly mice and teenagers, as these were all part of the target group. Matthew suggested creating a direct mail questionnaire on the free internet survey from **www.surveymonkey.com** and Millie thought this was a great idea.

The more raw data they had from the target market, the better the research would be. Millie's Mum was called in to help. She was asked to draw up a list of all her friends and carry out a telephone survey, which would also be part of the research findings.

Millie also put questionnaires together to help in the process. She found some useful tips and templates from the Internet on questionnaire development.

Matthew set up an administrative process to capture all the primary and secondary data in a meaningful way on an Excel spreadsheet. Millie monitored all the field work they had undertaken to ensure that the data collected was accurate. When the data was captured, they began to see trends emerging, not just in terms of what the target market wanted, but what they really needed.

They got some great ideas from the Focus Groups and the Internet Survey, because the target market liked being asked what they wanted, rather than being told what they needed.

Millie and Matthew could also see from their secondary research that 21st century companies follow a strategy that is all about customer profitability and **serving the customer**, rather than simply maximising sales. This led them to believe that successful companies require a 'thinking' rather than a 'doing' approach to business development. They needed to look at their customers as **Life Long Customers**, rather than looking for that one sale that brings in revenue to boost the shop takings.

Millie and Matthew came to the conclusion that if they created a strategy that focused entirely on their customers and aimed to exceed their expectations all of the time, this strategy would sustain The Cheese Mall long term.

They discovered that retaining a customer for life is smarter and makes more business sense, when you consider how long it takes and how much it costs to gain a new customer.

Millie and Matthew could see how undertaking the research had helped them to understand their target market of potential customers. They could also see how vital it was to have this information prior to starting a business. They realised that making assumptions about what potential customers want is a dangerous game and that it was important to drill down into the market and hear straight from the customers what their interests and needs are.

They were very surprised by what they had learned about market research. They had learned that market research is not just something you do when you are starting up a business; it needs to be an integral, ongoing part of a Business Development Strategy. They could also see that in the future, it would be crucial to research their target market before they spent time and money developing a new product or service.

Following the research, Millie and Matthew were more convinced that there was a real need in the market for a specialised Cheese

Mall in Mouseville. After their two weeks of research, they were more confident about making that call to the Mice People's Bank to set up an appointment to meet the Head Mouse Manager, Mr. Grudge.

CHAPTER 3
The Business Plan

Matthew slammed down the phone in anger.

"Mr Grudge won't meet us until we have a **Business Plan**," shouted Matthew.

"Calm down, Matthew," Millie said. "I thought this was going to happen. I know we said we would just meet him to see would he consider us for a loan, but if Mr. Grudge wants a Business Plan before he meets us, so be it."

"But we have never written a Business Plan before," Matthew replied.

"I know, but we have no choice; we have to do one. I think this is very positive, because we will have to do more background work, so at least we'll be prepared. It will be very good for us because writing the Business Plan will bring our idea to life."

Matthew came around to Millie's way of thinking and he agreed to take on the task of finding out exactly what was involved in putting a **Business Plan** together and what specific content was required. He was a bit scared about the whole idea of writing a Business

Plan, because he knew that once it was written and finances were secured, The Cheese Mall would be open for business. This frightened and excited him at the same time and he wondered whether Millie was feeling this way too.

He spent the whole day on the Internet, researching what makes a good Business Plan and downloading some really excellent Business Plan templates free of charge from Enterprise Boards and banks. He found **www.businessballs.com** particularly helpful, as it offered many free resources on every aspect of business. He also found the website **www.entrepreneur.com** very useful and **www.slideshare.net** offered free downloads of PowerPoint presentations.

He was amazed at how generous mice were in sharing their information and he promised himself that he would also share his knowledge. That evening he presented his findings to Millie.

He told her that the first page of the Business Plan would be called the **Executive Summary**, which in essence was a brief summary of the Business Plan. This should be no more than one page. The next chapter would be the **Introduction & Background**, which included company details and the purpose of the Business Plan. In their case, the purpose of their Business Plan was to seek funding from the Mice People's Bank to open The Cheese Mall.

The next chapter would be the **Project Outline**, which was a more detailed description of the proposed business. This also included their Mission Statement, trends in the industry and information on their target market.

The **Ownership, Management & Employment** section would follow on from that. This section provided background on the owners, their education, business experience, strengths, etc. Employment referred to the number of mice they would employ, how many would be full-time and how many would be part-time.

Matthew saw the worried look on Millie's face, but he pressed on. Having spent the day researching the Business Plan, he also saw the real benefits for them and their business in putting it together. The next chapter would be the **Market Research** section; he winked at

Millie, knowing that they had already completed their primary and secondary research. This section would also give an in-depth analysis of all their main competitors in the market.

The next chapter would be **Marketing Strategy**, which would look at what core products they would be presenting to the market place. It would look at what pricing structure would be in place and outline their Marketing Communications Strategy. There would be a SWOT Analysis in this section, which Matthew said he would explain later.

The next chapter would centre on **Strategic Objectives**, which would need to cover the following 3-6 Months, 6-12 Months and 12-36 months. While it was their intention to concentrate on cheese and associated products, they still had to implement Quality Controls and Health & Safety regulations.

Finally, the most important chapter of all would be the **Financial Statements**, which had to include Projected Performance, Cash Flow, Balance Sheet, Profit & Loss Account, and Funding Requirements.

Millie was not happy about the level of information needed for the plan and felt that

The Cheese Mall would never happen if they had to write all this information down. Matthew reassured her that it was indeed necessary that they do all this now. He explained that the Business Plan would not only help them to get the necessary funding, it would also help in providing a strategic direction for the business for the next three years.

When Millie calmed down, she accepted what Matthew had said and could see that the Business Plan would be like a road map. She could see what Matthew was getting at when he said that they would have to set their goals and more importantly, write them down and show how they were going to achieve them.

She was scared about the fact that once the Business Plan was written and finance secured, The Cheese Mall would be open for business. She was both frightened and excited and she wondered whether Matthew was feeling this way also.

Matthew thought it was best that they finish for the night and he would explain the Marketing Audit tomorrow. Their mother came in with much needed refreshments and they sat down and told her all about the detail that was required for the Business Plan.

Millie started to fret again and felt that with all this detail they had to go into, they would never get the business off the ground. Matthew reassured Millie that the Business Plan would provide the platform for them to make decisions with regard to the viability of the business.

Millie and Matthew could see the relief on their mother's face. They knew she was thinking that when they wrote it all down and worked through the financials and loan requirements, they would come to their senses and realise that The Cheese Mall was too big an undertaking for them to take on.

They knew that their Dad thought this way too. This gave them the impetus that they needed to go forward and their resolve increased. They were going to write the Business Plan and establish the business case for The Cheese Mall and prove that it was indeed a viable business.

CHAPTER 4
The Marketing Audit

The next morning, Millie and Matthew were up bright and early and were eager to start working on the development of their Business Plan. Matthew agreed to work on the Marketing Audit, while Millie agreed to meet the Finance Mouse, Mr. Catfish. They needed to get some advice on the financials which they had worked on over the past two weeks.

She was delighted he could fit her in that very morning. Mr. Catfish was recommended to them by their Dad, as he had previously worked at the Cheese Factory, but had left to start up his own business two years ago. According to their Dad, he was doing very well. He was busier than ever, as a lot of mice were thinking about starting out on their own following the recent announcement of redundancies at the Cheese Factory. Matthew and Millie were praying each night that no other mouse had the same ideas as they had for The Cheese Mall.

Before Millie left to visit Mr. Catfish, Matthew explained to her that he was going to start the Marketing Audit with a **SWOT Analysis**. He outlined the purpose of the SWOT Analysis to Millie, who found it fascinating. Matthew himself found it boring and saw it purely as a task to be completed. For the life of him, he could not see what fascination it held for Millie.

He informed Millie that a SWOT Analysis was a strategic planning tool that companies used to assess their **Strengths, Weaknesses, Opportunities and Threats**. It was all about identifying the internal and external factors that were favourable and unfavourable to achieving the objectives set by their business.

Strengths & Weaknesses referred to what goes on inside the business to help the company recognise what they were particularly good at (Strengths) and what areas they needed to work on (Weaknesses) to meet the needs of its target market.

The **Opportunities & Threats**, on the other hand, was an external analysis of the environment, which the company had no real control over. Although Millie looked a bit confused, Matthew said that it would all become very clear when he carried out their own SWOT Analysis for The Cheese Mall.

Millie said she would leave the SWOT Analysis in his capable hands and headed off to see Mr. Catfish. Their mother was going with Millie, as she had a background in finance. There would be no doubt that she would want to see the figures and go through them forensically before she and her Dad were convinced that this would be a viable business for them.

Matthew started writing down the internal **Strengths** of The Cheese Mall. He listed things like capabilities, competitive advantage, unique selling point, assets, experience, knowledge, advantage of their location, pricing strategy, quality accreditations, processes, systems, IT, marketing communications and brand image. He hadn't realised that they actually had a lot of strengths which they could build on.

Next, he looked at their internal **Weaknesses** for example gaps in capabilities, lack of competitive strength and reputation, low market share, high overheads, loan repayments, low cash flow and the fact that the business needed time to establish itself and to establish its brand. Matthew was not really sure what branding actually meant in relation to The Cheese Mall, but he included it anyway because he knew it was important and was something that they would have to work on.

Matthew then focused on the **Opportunities** (in the market place), looking at their competitors' vulnerabilities, industry and lifestyle trends, technology development, global influences, niche target markets, distribution, complementary products and currency fluctuations. He smiled at how currency fluctuations would benefit the business, as the DollarMouse was way ahead of the EuroCat.

Finally, he looked at **Threats** (in the market place). He knew he had no control over them, but they had to be listed so that they could show the Bank that they understood the external market in which they were operating.

He listed the main threat as competitors and also listed political and legislative demands, environmental factors, market demand and change in consumer tastes. He had read on the Internet that for health reasons, some mice were reducing their cheese intake and eating more fruit and even dark chocolate. How healthy was that? Anyway, changes in consumer tastes had to be listed and perhaps it presented an opportunity also to offer similar products at The Cheese Mall.

When Matthew finished the SWOT Analysis, he was very proud of himself and knew that Millie would immediately see a whole snapshot of The Cheese Mall. In his commentary on the SWOT Analysis for the Business Plan, he wrote that they would build on their Strengths to take advantage of the Opportunities in the market place.

They would always be mindful of their Threats and would do whatever they needed to do to eliminate the Weaknesses. Matthew knew they had control over the Weaknesses in their business and was confident that they could take action to overcome them.

As he typed the last sentence, Millie walked into the room, looking very pleased with herself. He handed her the SWOT Analysis and she studied it carefully. She could not believe that this was their business she was reading about. The SWOT Analysis explained very clearly what they needed to do and where the threats and opportunities were for them in the market place. She congratulated Matthew, which made him feel really chuffed with himself. He was beginning to see their business unfold and it felt good.

"The Finance Mouse," Matthew said. "I'm afraid to ask - how did you get on with Mr. Catfish?"

Millie beamed. "He was very happy with the projections and costings that Mum helped us with. And would you believe Matthew, even Mum is starting to come around - she's not looking so worried. He was also delighted with our market research and about our plans to promote ourselves in surrounding areas like Felixtown, Bugsville and Tomtown."

"Had he any concerns?" Matthew asked.

"Well, he was concerned about the amount of competitors we had in the market and about how we were going to be able to stand out from the crowded market. I told him not to worry, because we would have it all worked out in the promotional strategy in the Business Plan."

"How was Mum after the meeting?" Matthew asked.

"Well, like I say, more relaxed but still not 100% convinced," Millie replied. "And probably won't be until she sees the final Business Plan. Let's take a break for lunch, Matthew - we need to knuckle down now and create The Cheese Mall brand."

Matthew smiled at his twin's enthusiasm and energy. He was smiling a lot these days and so was Millie, but he wondered whether this was just the calm before the storm. He was becoming more excited than frightened now and he was wondering whether Millie was feeling the same.

CHAPTER 5
Market Segmentation

At lunch, all the talk was about the meeting with Mr. Catfish. Their Dad had come home from the Cheese Factory for lunch. This was most unusual for him, because he always wanted to stay in work just in case he was needed to fill an emergency order. However on this day, he could not wait until he got home to find out how the meeting went with the Finance Mouse.

He wasn't really listening to Millie going on excitedly about how impressed Mr. Catfish was with their idea. He kept looking at his wife, because he knew she was more grounded. When she confirmed what Millie was saying, he felt both relieved and anxious. He had still hoped that they would see sense and get themselves a real job.

After lunch, Millie and Matthew took over the second sitting room, which they had turned into their official HQ for The Cheese Mall. Millie switched on her laptop and pulled up some information she had researched on the Internet. She looked over at Matthew and said to him that she had been reading up on **Market Segmentation** and that it was very important for them to understand that a product or service that tries to appeal to everyone ends up appealing to no one.

Matthew did not fully understand what she was talking about and asked her what market segmentation had to do with The Cheese Mall.

"Quite a lot actually," said Mille. "Let me explain."

Millie explained that market segmentation was a marketing technique that targeted a group of customers with specific characteristics. Not all customers were the same, so no matter what business you were in, customers needed to be defined by segments. Market segmentation was the key ingredient for successful marketing, as it simplified the targeting, the positioning and the planning process.

"I'm totally confused now," said Matthew.

Millie could not understand why Matthew could not see this immediately, like she could. She could see the many benefits for companies who segmented their customers, as this helped them better understand their customers' exacting needs and wants. It also resulted in better targeting and positioning of a product and service.

To make the concept relevant to Matthew, Millie used The Cheese Mall as an example. His eyes lit up and he became more interested.

The Cheese Mall would have a variety of customers calling in each day. This could be considered the mass market, but individual groups will have individual needs.

She explained that **'Elderly'** mice shoppers would want friendly staff with time to talk to them. **'Fast'** mice shoppers wanted to be in and out as quick as possible for their bottle of wine, cheese and crackers, so express cash points would be vital.

'Professional' or **'Time Poor'** mice shoppers would want to buy all their cheese from the same shop, so they would want a wide variety of quality products. **'Mum' and 'Dad'** mice wanted value for money. The History of Cheese museum would entertain the kiddie mice while their parents browse. **'Teenagers'** would want a place to hang out, so a cafe would be good for them.

"So I hope you now realise that not all shoppers are the same," Millie said.

"I get it," Matthew replied. "What you are really saying is that if we go out with just one message, we could be alienating a particular group or segment as you call them. So we have to create a message that takes the needs of all the individual mice shoppers into account and make sure that message is included in our promotional material."

"You catch on fast, brother. There is no point in creating a brochure about all the wonderful exotic cheeses and wine we stock because this only resonates with the professional mice."

"I know what you're saying, Millie. This message would alienate other customers who may not be looking for exotic cheese and just want a nice place to shop."

"You have it in one, Matthew. By understanding market segmentation it will help us put the customer at the centre of everything we do and this philosophy and way of doing business will drive the whole **Marketing Mix**."

Matthew was starting to get really excited, because their idea was now coming to life.

"Have I got it right, Millie? In our research, we identified our target market and their location, so now what we need to do is look at our target market and start to segment it."

"That's right," Millie replied.

"In other words, we have to try to work out how many Elderly, Professional, Married and Teenage mice we have in each geographical area. Once we have this done, we can start looking at our **Marketing Communications**. But before we do this, can you just explain to me briefly what you mean by the Marketing Mix?"

Millie was in her element again, because she had also discovered through her Internet research the importance of the Marketing Mix for any business. She explained that it was made up of five key elements – **Product, Price, Promotion, Place and People – the 5 Ps of Marketing as it is often referred to as**. She had found out that if a business was not working and you wanted to find out where it was going wrong, you would find the answer in one of the 5 Ps.

"Are you joking?" Matthew asked.

"No, I'm deadly serious," said Millie. "We might get four of the elements right, but if we fall down on one of them, it will pull the other four down with it. Let me explain."

She outlined that a **Product** was anything that could satisfy a need or a want. It could be 'tangible' (see, touch, hear, smell or taste) or 'intangible' for example a service. The product had to deliver the benefits and meet customer expectations. It was important to get the product right because this was where the revenue comes from. Companies needed to listen to their market feedback, which measured customer satisfaction with their product.

Price involved the amount of money exchanged for the product. To the buyer, it meant the value placed on the product. It was also important to include the 'value-added' in a way that the customer would understand.

"What do you mean by 'value added' Millie?" Matthew asked.

"'Value added' means additional benefits that a customer receives beyond price, like variety, opening hours, customer service, quality, brand guarantee, etc."

"So what you are saying," Matthew said, "is that the more value-added benefits you give a customer, the more satisfied they are with the price."

"Exactly," Millie responded. "It's also very important to charge what the market can take. What I mean by this is that the market dictates the price. I was reading somewhere that when mice start out in business, they tend to charge a price that they think is reasonable, rather than what the market can take, because they haven't done any research on what their competitors are charging."

"I don't understand," Matthew replied. "Why would you charge more if it covers your costs and you are happy enough with the price you are getting?"

"The reason is that the price has already been determined by the market, which in essence is our customers," said Millie. "They are prepared to pay a particular price for a product because of all the added value associated with it. There will be high profit products, but we will also be stocking low profit products so the two products will balance each other out."

"I get you now. It makes sense to listen to the market when we're determining our pricing and checking out our competitors. We'll also be mindful of margins and profits. We have so much to learn, but we are getting there, Millie."

Millie went on to outline the third element of the Marketing Mix, **Promotion**. This referred to how a company communicated with both existing and potential customers. They could use four key mediums, or ways of communicating: (i) Direct Marketing; (ii) Internet Marketing; (iii) Networking and (iv) Advertising & PR (Public Relations).

"I get it," said Matthew. "This is our **Marketing Communications Strategy.**"

"That's correct," Millie replied. "Top of the class."

The fourth element was **Place**, which referred to how goods reach the customer and how quickly, for example, a 'Distribution Strategy'. In their case, their proposed structure or channels of distribution for The Cheese Mall was through the retail store.

Their current plan was to buy their product from intermediaries, for example, cheese wholesalers. They could decide to go direct to the manufacturer in the future, but it would all depend on volumes and whether it was best to buy from two or three large wholesalers, rather than from a number of small artisan producers, which would increase administrative and operational costs. Under their current distribution strategy, they would need to establish stock control systems, transport and storage, etc.

Place also referred to their retail store and the importance of the shop interior, layout, ambiance, cleanliness and shop window, not to mention ease of parking and the general environment of the area where the shop was located. Signage that made it easy for their customers to find them was another important element of Place.

The last element was **People**. "Does this mean the customers we are selling to?" Matthew asked.

"No," Millie replied. "People refer to the mice staff we will employ in the business."

Millie explained that this was one of the most important elements of the Marketing Mix, because if customers had a bad experience with retail staff, they would not return, no matter how wonderful the products were or how lovely the shop interior was. This would reflect very negatively on the brand promise.

"What do you mean by brand promise?" Matthew asked.

Millie explained that a **brand promise** was created by advertising and promotion activities, whereas the brand delivery encompassed everything customers experience when they were actually dealing with the brand. Quality of products and service was critical, but the attitude and behaviour of the front-line staff was more important in the eyes of customers. The brand promise painted a picture of what customers would experience, but the **brand delivery** referred to the experience itself.

"I hope this explains why People are such a key element of the Marketing Mix," Millie said.

"It sure does," Matthew replied. "It's very important that we recruit the right mice. Recruiting the wrong mice for The Cheese Mall would mean that everything we're doing right now to build the brand would be in vain, because the 'brand delivery' would be at risk. Gosh, Millie, People seems to be the most difficult element of the Marketing Mix."

"If we want to do all that we said we would do to make The Cheese Mall a success, we need to recruit," said Millie firmly.

They had both learned from their experience in the Cheese Factory how not to manage - the only time they ever heard from their manager was when they did something wrong. Their managers were never there to acknowledge when they did something right.

They understood that in order for their business to survive, they needed to have meaningful engagement with their mice employees to ensure that they maintained their market share and increased customer loyalty and retention.

"It's very important for us to understand that we need to set an example," said Millie seriously. "The way we treat our mice employees will reflect how our mice employees treat our customers."

"I agree 100%," Matthew replied. "Let's call it a day, Millie. We'll need all our energies tomorrow to start building The Cheese Mall brand under our **Marketing Communications Strategy**."

"I can't wait," said Millie.

"Me neither. I probably won't be able to sleep, because there will be so many ideas going around in my head. I might have a BudMouse before I go to bed."

"Only one," Millie smiled. "I don't want any big head in the morning - we have work to do."

"Maybe two," Matthew laughed.

Millie smiled to herself as Matthew switched off his laptop. She felt really positive, but wondered whether this was just the calm before the storm. She was more excited than frightened now and she was wondering whether Matthew was feeling the same.

CHAPTER 6
Building a Brand

"I always thought it was only the large companies that could develop brands," Matthew said to Millie as they started their working day. "I couldn't sleep, so I got up very early and started doing research of my own. It was only when I was reading up on the whole area of branding that I realised that small companies can also create brands."

"How do they do that?" Millie asked.

"It's not as complex as some marketing mice make it out to be."

Matthew outlined to Millie that **Branding** was sometimes described as the DNA of a business. The objective of branding was that it attracted a group of customers who are 'brand loyal' and if a company delivered on the brand promise, customers would buy the brand regularly and would not change to competitor brands easily.

The benefit for the customer was that they could identify with the company and their reputation for quality and would feel secure when parting with their money. **Branding** also helped a company to introduce a new product, because consumers were already familiar with the company's existing brands. Psychologically, brands satisfied security needs. For example, buying designer label clothes or a particular brand of car meant the mouse was looking to the brand to provide them with the benefit of being socially acceptable.

"Are brands that powerful?" Millie asked.

"Absolutely," Matthew replied. "That's why companies invest so much time and money in protecting their brand image. They reward brand loyalty with gifts like frequent flyer points or loyalty cards at cheese supermarkets."

"Will we have to do this as well, you know, put in some loyalty card system for our mice customers?" Millie asked.

"Let's talk about that later, when we look at Marketing Communications," Matthew replied. "I just want to fill you in further on the importance of branding for our business."

Matthew explained that companies would go to the highest courts to protect their brand image. Advertisers gave brands a personality which could either be serious like a bank, or fun like Disneyland, which had the biggest mouse brands, Mickey and Minnie Mouse.

"Wouldn't it be great if we got them to officially open The Cheese Mall?" Millie said.

"Forget it, Millie, these guys do not get out of bed for less than a million a day," said Matthew. "But they do us proud as brand ambassadors."

Matthew explained that a brand was the source of a promise to the customer. Everything a company did needed to be focused on enhancing delivery against their brand's promise. In summary, the brand was the glue that held all the marketing functions together.

"When brand communication comes through intact – crystal clear and potent – it goes straight into mice's brains without distortion, noise or the need to think too much about it," said Matthew.

"It will be so important to get our branding right," Millie said, looking a bit concerned. "How are we going to do that?"

"Of course, we'll have to work on it Millie," Matthew replied. "But if we put the customer at the centre of everything we do, then we're destined for success. I don't mean to be over-confident here, but our brand will be the source of the promise we make to our customer."

Matthew was amazed to read that really good branding could pre-sell products before they were even launched. It was all about the customer and their needs and wants.

When it came to positioning The Cheese Mall brand, they would have to create an image that would resonate with their target market.

"How are we going to do this?" Millie asked.

"Put simply, Millie, we have to ask ourselves what business we are in."

"The cheese business, of course."

"No, it goes further than that. All our competitors sell cheese; we will be selling a retail experience."

"Well, I know that, but our customers are coming in for the cheese."

"That's not entirely true, with the possible exception of some specialist cheeses, which may be unique to The Cheese Mall. The standard cheeses and products they can buy in all the other stores. So what makes our cheese special is the shopping experience."

"I can see what you are getting at, Matthew."

"We go the extra mile," said Matthew. "As you explained to me before, we do this because we add value. We will have a cafe on site for them to rest, a bookstore with cheese cookery books, a cookery school and in-store demonstrations. We will have the Cheese Museum for the kids as well – I could go on and on showing how we are different. So we're not just selling cheese, you understand; we're selling a retail experience."

"I get it," Millie clapped her hands. "Here am I thinking that mice are coming in for the product. Because we've put so much energy into creating a product offering that's different, they will shop with us and become loyal to our brand. We will be giving them what they asked for in the research, which will send a clear signal to our target market that we listened."

"Go on, Millie, I'm impressed," Matthew teased.

"So we're not creating a shop that we think the market wants, we are creating a shop that the market has told us it wants. Why did I not see this before? So this is what you mean when you say we put the customer at the centre of everything that we do, because it means we've listened and developed our brand around what they told us they wanted. Fantastic, Matthew, you are a genius."

"It's our customers who are geniuses, Millie. They created The Cheese Mall and I can tell you now, the more we listen to them as we develop our business, the more successful we will be."

Matthew ended by talking about the time he did some work experience in a Cheese Store on Whisker Street. While he was there, he suggested a Customer Survey to find out what the customers really wanted from them. They said to him that they knew what their customers wanted. Matthew now knew that what they really meant to say was: 'we know what we want.' At the time, he did not realise this, but now he was more than ever convinced about the importance of customer engagement at every level of the business.

"Now, let's get to work on our **Marketing Communications**, Millie," he said enthusiastically.

CHAPTER 7
Marketing Communications

Millie took over the conversation, as she had researched the four key elements of **Marketing Communications**. She outlined these as (i) Direct Marketing; (ii) Internet Marketing, (iii) Networking and (iv) Advertising & PR (Public Relations). They had to do all of these, all of the time in order to have any meaningful engagement with their customers.

Millie knew that Matthew would only be interested in one medium, Internet Marketing. He was convinced that if they put in place a really good Internet Marketing Strategy that was all they would need.

Millie quashed this thought by explaining that Internet Marketing was just one medium; if they ignored the other three, they would do so at their peril. She suggested that they look at each one and decide what action they would take in each area.

She began with **Direct Marketing**. Now that they had identified the segments they could set about doing up a brochure which would appeal to all of the segments. They had to be very careful about identifying the needs of each segment. She reminded Matthew that an elderly mouse's needs were different from those of a working mouse, mother mouse, etc. Their brochure would be delivered to homes in the target area, so it had to reflect the different needs of each segment.

She pointed out that **'Benefits'** sell, so they spent a lot of time listing all the reasons why mice should shop in their store. She showed Matthew a list of key words which needed to be included in the brochure, because they are powerful emotional words and emotion sells.

These included words like Easy, Save, Love, Health, You, Your, Free, New, Money, Results, Proven, Guarantee. Using these words really helped them to draw up a list of key benefits.

They then worked on the **'Features'** – they listed all the products and services they were offering.

Millie reminded Matthew that Features only accounted for 20% of the purchase decision, so it was very important that Benefits, which account for 80% of the purchase decision, were very much to the fore in the brochure.

As this was their first Direct Mail to their customers, Millie suggested a discount coupon in the brochure so that they could see how effective the mailing was. Matthew thought this was a great idea.

They spent hours working on the content, but when it was finished it was worth every minute. This was their first direct marketing communication with their customer. It had to be 100%. Anything less than that was unacceptable, as it would impact negatively on their brand.

Matthew's friend Cecil was working on the logo and they were both looking forward to seeing it the next day.

Millie and Matthew were too excited to finish up, so they started on their **Internet Marketing Strategy**. They needed a website. Matthew was on to this. He looked at all their competitors' websites and wrote down what was good and not so good about each of them. It was critical that they got this right, as their website was their virtual shop and would speak volumes about their brand.

Initially, Matthew had wanted to build his own website, but Millie was having none of it - she wanted a proper e-commerce website. Matthew came around to the idea and while his ego was a bit dented, he knew Millie was right.

Matthew insisted that they needed a business presence on the social media websites **www.facebook.com** and on **www.twitter.com**. He also suggested the professional site **www.linkedin.com**. He also wanted to put up a video giving a virtual tour of the shop on **www.youtube.com** and set up a YouTube channel to put up some cookery demonstrations.

Millie clapped her hands in delight as she visualised it all. Matthew said that he would also look into affiliated sites. He had already met the web designer and discussed the whole area of Search Engine Optimisation (SEO), as it was important they get the traffic to the website. Matthew also outlined to Millie the importance of having many 'calls to action' on the site.

"What does this mean?" Millie asked.

"It just means that no matter where the user is on the site, it should be easy for them to buy," Matthew replied.

Matthew was glad they had decided to get a professional website designer in the end, because there was a lot he did not know about building a website from a marketing perspective.

Millie said that she would start a Blog through the WordPress website **www.wordpress.com** and link it to their website and the other social media sites. She would try to get as many followers as possible, because she liked writing and liked the idea of sharing her experiences of running the shop with other budding entrepreneurs.

Matthew thought this was a great idea but smiled to himself, wondering when Millie would get the time to write the blog. Nonetheless, he went along with her.

As often happens with twins, Millie knew what Matthew was thinking. She sensed that Matthew was not convinced and reassured him that she would find the time. This was a powerful medium of communication with customers and it was free, so it would have been crazy to ignore it.

It was after midnight and they were exhausted. They decided to head off to bed and resume in the morning to discuss Networking and Advertising and PR. Matthew was convinced that it would be enough just to focus on Direct Marketing and Internet Marketing. Millie insisted that he wait until she outlined the benefits of including these other two mediums in their Marketing Communications Strategy.

The next day, Matthew was up before Millie. This was a regular occurrence of late. In the past, their mother had to practically drag him out of the bed but now he just could not wait to get up. His mind was racing after all the things they discussed yesterday and he was really looking forward to seeing the logo today.

They recommenced at 08.00. Millie was tired; she hadn't slept so well because she kept thinking about different ideas. However, she got all energised again when she started talking about the power of **Networking**. She explained to Matthew that it was all about building relationships. The Networking platform would provide an opportunity for them to meet their prospective customers face to face.

Millie outlined the various types of networking open to them. They decided on the Mouseville Chamber of Commerce, the Retail Association of Mouseville, Bloggers Group and the Female Mice Entrepreneurs' Business Network. Matthew complained about the fact that there was no Male Mice Entrepreneurs' Business Network. Millie explained that male mice had good networking supports through their sporting activities. Matthew had never looked at it this way and could see where Millie was coming from.

Matthew agreed to join the local golf club and he was already a member of his local football and cricket clubs. Millie decided she would continue her membership of the local tennis club, as it would be good for them to have some work life balance in the form of sports. It would also provide valuable networking opportunities for them with their target market.

Millie also talked about the need for them both to spread the same message, with an **'elevator pitch.'**

"What is an elevator pitch?" Matthew asked.

Millie replied that it was a carefully planned and well-practiced description about their business that a baby mouse could understand. It would be delivered in the time it took to ride in an elevator – 30 seconds. The elevator pitch was important because it was the first thing that mice would hear about their business.

"We will have to work on this," she said, "but it would go something like 'we are in the business of providing our customers with the ultimate retail experience. In our shop, we have cheeses and complementary products from around the world, cheese tastings, exotic free recipes, a cafe to relax in and friendly staff to provide all the advice our customers need.'"

"I actually like this," said Matthew.

"Really, the purpose of this elevator pitch is to prompt the listener to ask more about the shop. If we just said we run a cheese store on Whisker Street, we would just sound like all the other retail stores in the area. So we have to excite them and bring our brand to life."

Matthew could see the benefits of being different and saying something that would hook the potential customer in. He did not want to be a follower because he knew if they just followed it would all come down to who was the cheapest in the end.

He liked the elevator pitch and was looking forward to delivering it with pride at a network meeting or conference, workshop or even on the football pitch.

Matthew's mobile rang. It was Cecil. He had just sent over the email with the logo attachment. Matthew indicated that he was with Millie and they would have a look at it and get back to him. Both of them looked at each other. The Cheese Mall was about to be brought to life through this symbol.

It was both scary and exciting. They didn't doubt that Cecil would deliver, because he was very good at what he did. The reason why they were apprehensive was because they had spent so much time over the past few days talking about their brand and what they wanted it to symbolise.

Before Matthew opened the document, Millie told him about the time the Cheese Factory changed from its traditional symbol to a contemporary one. The management got so many complaints from customers about the new symbol that they contemplated going back to the original logo. Unfortunately, because they had spent so much money on the rebranding and it was on their packaging, their brochures, they decided to leave it. They obviously did not care or understand how their customers viewed their original symbol; they just ignored them.

Matthew opened his email account and saw the email from Cecil. They already had a brand personality of their own in mind and they were hoping that Cecil had captured the essence of that personality in the logo.

He looked at Millie. She nodded and he opened the email. There was no message, just the attachment. Matthew clicked on the attachment. It opened up in jpeg format and filled the whole screen. Matthew and Millie just stared at it, mesmerised.

Matthew slapped his leg and said "He's done it. It's fantastic."

Millie squealed with delight. "He must have been listening to us talking for the last few days."

The symbol immediately resonated with them and they both knew it was the one for them.

"We can get our stationery organised now and include business cards," Millie said, her eyes gleaming. "I'll contact Cecil and get some pricing around design and printing. This logo will look fantastic on our brochure. It ties in with our brand essence, creating that ultimate retail experience. I can just see it on the shop front."

"I can see it on the website, the Facebook page, all over the Internet," Matthew said excitedly. "It will be such a talking point. It's truly amazing."

"We need a tag line," Millie said.

"A what?"

"A tag line is a slogan that captures our essence. We have the logo, then the name 'The Cheese Mall' and then underneath the name, the tag line could be something like 'the ultimate retail experience.'"

"I love it," Matthew shouted. "The Cheese Mall is now open for business and there is no turning back now."

Millie distracted Matthew by turning to the final element of the Promotional Strategy, which was **Advertising and PR**. They did not have big money, but they needed to advertise, so they decided that they would focus on the local newspapers and local newsletters in the different target towns, rather than go national. They agreed on the publications to approach and divided the task of getting some prices for the advertising spend.

Millie came up with a great idea to do a feature alongside the advertisement with a headline 'The Twins are doing it for themselves'. She believed they had a real story to tell of how they lost their job, decided to follow a dream and learn so much about themselves and business in making this journey.

Millie felt that this would be a real inspiration to budding entrepreneurs, because they had started off with very little knowledge and here they were a few weeks' later, building a brand, writing a Business Plan and more importantly, creating a blueprint for the future success of the business.

She could not wait to tell the budding entrepreneurs that it was all about the customer and if they put the customer at the centre of everything that they did; their brand and Business Plan would fall into place very easily.

Matthew liked this idea of a 'mouse interest story'. He could see the benefits of getting a full page spread, because mice loved a story.

Matthew thought it was very clever how Millie was using the story to get the brand out there in such a subtle way, because it was bringing the brand to life. It was important that their customers had an affinity with them as the business owners, because mice buy from mice at the end of the day.

"I like it," Matthew said. "Let's do it. You know, we might even get some coverage in the national newspapers and the business shows on the radio. They all want a good news story about mice taking a risk and 'doing it for themselves.'"

CHAPTER 8
Strategic Objectives

Millie and Matthew spent the next few days pulling the Business Plan together and capturing all the information they needed for Mr. Grudge, the Mouse Bank Manager. Having created most of the content through brain storming, it was easy to include what they needed to get the business up and running.

They had got costings from the Mouse House Agents for the vacant shop on Whisker Street. It was perfect for The Cheese Mall, as they had use of the upstairs as well. They got prices for shop fittings, stocks, rates, insurances, everything that was needed.

When the Finance Mouse provided them with the final spreadsheet required for the overall loan, their little hearts fluttered. This was the first time they had spoken openly to each other about their true fears.

"This is a big loan, Matthew," Millie said. "It is going to take us some time to build up the business and break even."

"I know, Millie."

"We're going to have to work very hard and to be honest, I am a bit scared. Sometimes I go from being really excited about The Cheese Mall to wishing I had never started it."

"But we have come so far. We can't just give up."

"I'm not talking about giving up. All I am saying is that we have to realise that this is a risk for all of us. Dad is putting up guarantees and we have to go in and convince a Bank Manager that we can run this business successfully when we have never run a business in our life. What do we know about retail? Now that's the scary bit for me. What about you?"

"Of course I feel the same fear as you do, but my real fear is all around failure."

"What do you mean, Matthew?"

"I just don't want to fail. I guess you can say my ego is getting in the way here, but the thought of failure scares me no end."

"Why do you think we'll fail?" Millie asked, feeling a little bit insecure.

"I know we have proven that there is a market for The Cheese Mall and I know that we can make it work. We'll work very hard. But what if we don't get the customers in? What if it doesn't work? What if we end up in debt for life?"

"It will be an emotional journey on all levels, Matthew. We need more than a Business Plan to make it work. We need to believe in ourselves and to understand that we will meet many obstacles along the way, but we will address these as they arise, one step at a time."

"I am so glad we're talking openly, Millie. There were times during these last weeks when I was feeling scared and excited all at the same time and I was wondering how you were feeling."

"Funny you should say that, Matthew, I was feeling exactly the same way and I was wondering how you were feeling. I think these are natural jitters, we would not be normal mice if we did not feel threatened."

"You're right, Millie, it's best to put our fears on the table and deal with them as they arise. We can't run this business with our head in the sand."

"I agree," Millie replied. "We would not be normal mice if we did not indulge in some potential catastrophes, but at this moment in time, we have the evidence to prove that it will succeed. So let's get to work and finish this Business Plan - I'm sick looking at it."

They both laughed and it helped to ease their nerves. They sat in silence, waiting for their little hearts to return to normal levels. They looked up and smiled at one another and started the process of putting their key strategic objectives on paper.

"One thing always confuses me," Millie said. "What's the difference between a goal and an objective? Are they one and the same?"

"Not really," Matthew replied.

Matthew explained that a **Goal** was an outcome, an accomplishment. In order to set objectives, you have to set specific goals which are both realistic and achievable. The **Objectives** are the actions and steps required to achieve the Goal.

Matthew gave an example of how one of their key goals was the implementation of an 'Internet Marketing Strategy' for The Cheese Mall. This is the Goal and the Objectives refer to the way they are going to achieve the Goal.

"What we are doing now is working out our **Key Strategic Goals** which will set a direction for the business," Matthew said. "This is an ongoing process, because goals and objectives will change depending on what's going on out there in the market. This Business Plan has allowed us to step back and see the wood from the trees. It also forced us to challenge assumptions as an adhoc approach to business development is no longer appropriate."

"So first, we list the Goal and under that, we have three columns. The first column lays out WHAT needs to be done, for example, the steps required. The second column indicates WHO is going to do it and the third column indicates WHEN, for example, the completion date."

Matthew went on to explain that this part of the Business Plan had to be constantly reviewed. Because they had so many goals to achieve, both prior to the business starting and after it started up, they spent the rest of the day writing these down and assigning responsibilities. As this was a 3-Year Business Plan, they had to write goals and objectives to cover periods of 3-6 months, 6-12 months and 12-36 months.

They had good fun looking at where their business was going to be in three years. Millie talked about opening stores in every town, while Matthew suggested that they franchise the business out to other towns and let other up-and-coming entrepreneurial mice run them. One thing they knew for sure was that nothing and no one could limit their dreams, only themselves.

As the Business Plan was written for the purpose of funding, the goals in Year 3 had to be realistic. Their dreams were put on hold for the moment, but this was their ultimate vision for the business.

Satisfied with the list and the completion of the Business Plan, they turned off the light at 02.00 and went to bed. They knew they would not sleep very much, as tomorrow was their day of reckoning. They were meeting the Bank Manager, Mr. Grudge at 14.00. He would decide their ultimate fate with the stroke of a pen.

CHAPTER 9
The Day of Reckoning

Matthew and Millie sat quietly at the breakfast table. As predicted, they hadn't slept the night before. Yesterday had been about writing their strategic objectives, pulling the plan together and getting the final financials from the Finance Mouse.

Today was their day of reckoning.

They were satisfied with the final Business Plan and emailed it to Mr. Grudge early that morning so that he would have a copy in advance of their meeting. Their Dad had taken the day off work. He remarked that in such a short time, they had grown up and grasped the nettle. He was very proud of their achievements.

Their mother chimed in, saying that she could not believe that in such a short space of time, they had learned about their market and what they needed to do in order to make a real success of The Cheese Mall.

At 13.15, both of them were ready to go.

They looked good. Matthew had bought his first suit and Millie looked very smart as well.

They looked and felt like entrepreneurs embarking on a journey of self discovery. Their Dad wanted to drive them into the town for their appointment.

They both kissed their Mum goodbye and could see tears in her eyes. They understood that her tears were more about her worry that they would receive bad news after all their hard work. Mille and Matthew reassured her that no matter what decision was made, they would accept it.

They got into town very quickly and Millie kissed her Dad on the cheek and Matthew shook his hand. He looked concerned too, but again they knew he was worried about the disappointment they would feel if the decision did not go their way.

They got out of the car and stared up at the Mouse People's Bank. For the first time, they were overwhelmed by how big it was. They knew in their hearts that once the decision was made, regardless of the outcome, their lives would never be the same again.

They walked into the Bank and asked to see Mr. Grudge. They sat patiently, pretending to be calm. They made small talk, but were not really listening to one another. Millie smiled at Matthew and wished him good luck. He returned the smile and wished her the same.

Their little moment of calm was interrupted when Mr. Grudge appeared. He wasn't smiling. They had emailed the Business Plan that morning, which meant he had had plenty of time to analyse the data and the figures they had presented.

They all walked silently to his office. It was an unfriendly office, with no personal effects, just a glass desk and laptop. A copy of their Business Plan lay nakedly on his desk. They saw that it was underlined and highlighted and their little hearts began to flutter once again.

They had brought an original version with them, which was nicely bound. They handed it to Mr Grudge. He took it without comment and reverted to the email version. Then he looked back down at the Business Plan and scanned it briefly.

He looked up at them with a wide smile which didn't reach his eyes and said:

"I'm very impressed. Tell me honestly, who wrote this Business Plan for you?"

Millie and Matthew looked at each other in surprise. Then they burst out laughing, much to disapproval of Mr. Grudge. They got themselves into such a state of giggles that they could not stop. The laughter released all of the stress they had held in for the past few weeks and it was a great feeling. The more they looked at Mr. Grudge, the more they laughed. Finally, they regained their composure and Matthew spoke first, biting his lip to keep himself from laughing again.

"Mr. Grudge," he said feeling very chuffed with himself. "We wrote the Business Plan. Both Millie and I worked very hard and spent many late nights writing this together. It is all our own work and we would be happy to answer any questions you may have." He was afraid to look over at Millie in case she started laughing again.

Millie continued trying to sound serious but she couldn't keep the smirk from her face. "Your insistence on us providing you with the Business Plan prior to our meeting has been the best learning curve for us. It brought our business to life and because of our research it has convinced us even more that there is a market for what we are going to provide. We believe that we have proven the business case to you in our plan for The Cheese Mall."

Mr. Grudge looked down again at the email version of the plan and when he looked up, he had an even bigger smile on his face. This time it did reach his eyes.

"Well done," he said. "This has to be one of the best Business Plans I have ever read from a new business start-up. I am not only impressed with the financial content but with your own thinking and understanding of your market. It is very evident that you both know that you will only succeed in business when you put the customer at the centre of everything that you do. Knowing this will certainly help you to build a strong brand and a loyal customer base. Congratulations on a fine achievement; quite frankly, I am gobsmacked."

Millie and Matthew smiled at each other feeling very proud and emotional. They 'high fived' each other and Mr. Grudge also joined in with the 'high five'. It looked so comical, because he was just not the 'high five' type and the three of them started laughing.

"Let's get down to business," Mr. Grudge said in a more open and friendly manner. "So, Millie and Matthew, tell me more about all your wonderful plans for The Cheese Mall." They took up this invitation with great enthusiasm and pride.

Meanwhile, Dad fiddled at the radio. He couldn't concentrate on any of the radio programmes he listened to. He fiddled with the buttons, changing the stations constantly, but nothing held his attention. They had been in the bank for over an hour now. This was not a good sign, he thought sadly. If the Bank wanted to support his kids, it would only have been a case of rubber stamping the Business Plan.

Suddenly, he saw Millie's red suit and Matthew, looking so handsome in his new charcoal grey suit, as they came out of the main entrance. They were waving and beaming at him with delight, as they made their way towards his car. His spirits lifted and he beamed in anticipation. He knew it just had to be good news!!

His heart fluttered. "They've done it", he squeaked in delight.

They were now on the road to success and with hard work and a little bit of mouse luck, their dreams would come true. At this moment in time, he was the proudest mouse Dad on the planet.

******

Their Entrepreneurial Journey continues

Follow Millie and Matthew on
www.twitter.com/thecheesemall and
www.facebook.com/thecheesemall

Read Millie's Blog on
www.thecheesemall.wordpress.com

www.thecheesemall.com

www.ingramcontent.com/pod-product-compliance
Lightning Source LLC
Chambersburg PA
CBHW061516180526
45171CB00001B/202